COOL JOBS WITH...

JOBS

for

Young Entertainers

Ways to Make Money
Putting on an Event

Pam Scheunemann

ABDO
Publishing Company

Visit us at www.abdopublishing.com

Published by ABDO Publishing Company, 8000 West 78th Street, Edina, Minnesota 55439.
Copyright © 2011 by Abdo Consulting Group, Inc. International copyrights reserved in all countries.
No part of this book may be reproduced in any form without written permission from the publisher.
The Checkerboard Library™ is a trademark and logo of ABDO Publishing Company.

Printed in the United States , North Mankato, Minnesota
052010
092010

 PRINTED ON RECYCLED PAPER

Design and Production: Kelly Doudna, Mighty Media, Inc.
Series Editor: Liz Salzmann
Photo Credits: Kelly Doudna, iStockPhoto (Ana Abejon, Digital Skillet Photography, Jack Hollingsworth, Leah-Anne Thompson, Murat Giray Kaya), Shutterstock
Money Savvy Pig® photo courtesy of Money Savvy Generation/www.msgen.com

**Library of Congress
Cataloging-in-Publication Data**

Scheunemann, Pam, 1955-
  Cool jobs for young entertainers : ways to make money putting on an event / Pam Scheunemann.
     p. cm. -- (Cool kid jobs)
  Includes index.
  ISBN 978-1-61613-199-9
  1. Money-making projects for children--Juvenile literature.
2. Entertainers--Vocational guidance--Juvenile literature. 3. Success in business--Juvenile literature. 4. Finance, Personal --Juvenile literature. I. Title.
  HF5392.S346 2011
  791--dc22
                    2010004319

NOTE TO ADULTS

A job can be a good learning experience for you and your child. Be sure to encourage your child to discuss his or her job ideas with you. Talk about the risks and the benefits. Set up some rules for your child's safety with regard to:

* working with strangers

* transportation to and from the job

* proper and safe use of tools or equipment

  giving out phone numbers or e-mail addresses

* emergency contacts

Contents

Why Have an Event?

There are a lot of reasons to put on an event. The first one you probably think of is to earn money. But you can get more out of it than just money. You can learn new skills, meet new people, and get some experience.

MAKING MONEY

Your event can provide a fun experience for your **audience**. If your show is well-attended, you can earn some money!

BESIDES MONEY

You will gain more than money when you plan an event. You also get experience and learn about being responsible. That means planning carefully and doing what you agreed to do.

Volunteering is doing a job you don't get paid for. But you can earn other rewards. You can learn new skills that will help you get other jobs. And you can feel good about helping out!

What Can You Do with Your Money?

There are four things you can do with the money you earn.

SAVE

Saving is keeping your money in a safe place. You add money a little at a time as you earn it. Soon you could save enough for something such as a new bike.

SPEND

Spending is using your money to buy things you want. Maybe you want to go to a movie or buy a new computer game.

DONATE

It is important to give some of your earnings to organizations that help others.

INVEST

Investing is saving for long-term goals such as college expenses.

Ask your parents to help you decide how much money to use for each purpose. You'll be glad you did!

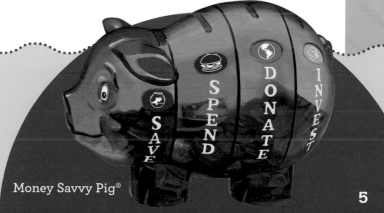

Money Savvy Pig®

What's Your Plan?

Planning carefully for your event is very important. The amount of planning that goes into an event really shows! It can be the difference between making and losing money. Without planning, there can be mix-ups. Some things might not get done on time. So plan, plan, plan!

WHO WILL DO THE PLANNING?

Who is going to work with you on the event? Is it a group of your friends? How about your brothers or sisters? Will you all have equal say, or is there one person in charge? Think about having an adult around to give you advice.

GET PERMISSION

Before you begin, make sure you have permission. There are many parts to putting on an event. You might need to paint **props**, make costumes, or hang curtains. You need permission to do these types of things. Ask before you use things you find around the house!

WHAT IS YOUR EVENT?

Once you've decided who is going to help out, choose the type of event. Below is a list of ideas for various events. But there are many other possibilities too. You might have a great idea that is completely different!

* backyard carnival
* talent show
* play or skit
* music concert
* dance recital
* haunted house
* magic show
* puppet show
* karate show
* fashion show
* variety show

WHERE WILL THE EVENT TAKE PLACE?

You will need a place to hold your event. Think about what kind of space you need. Do you need a stage? Do you need stage curtains? Is any part of your event messy? How many people do you think will come? Will you need seating for an **audience**? Some ideas for locations include:

* garage
* basement
* backyard
* party room
* living room
* community center
* place of worship

WHEN WILL YOU HOLD THE EVENT?

Pick a day when all the planners and helpers are free. Also, make sure you can use the location that day. Do you have enough time to set up? Is it a time when your **audience** can attend? Will you hold the event more than once?

WILL YOU NEED EXTRA HELP?

Will you need more people than those doing the event planning? Think carefully about everything that needs to be done. You might need people to:

* make **props** and backdrops
* make posters and signs
* plan games
* provide prizes for the games
* act, sing, or dance
* provide music
* make or buy tickets to sell
* sell the tickets to the audience
* get money to make change
* provide and sell **refreshments**
* keep track of the money
* clean up after the event

TRY TO THINK OF EVERYTHING

Don't just plan for what you want to happen at your event. Also consider what could go wrong. How would you handle any problems?

Theater Schedule

Show Dates April 23 & 24

Meetings will be held on Tuesday and Saturday afternoons.

Date	What	Who
2-Feb	Get together to select a show. Determine committees needed.	
9-Feb	Make committee assignments	Everyone
15-Feb	Select actors for roles	Everyone
20-Feb	**FIRST COMMITTEE MEETINGS**	Jenny & David
20-Feb	Rehearsal	Director & Actors
20-Feb	Advertising committee meets to plan for tickets/flyers/banners	Monica, Rob, Ben
20-Feb	Concessions committee develops plan	Jane, Ed, Ronda, Mary
20-Feb	Budget committee meets to form a budget	Diana, Rick, Monica
20-Feb	Costume committee meets	Sandy, Gwen, Paige
20-Feb	Sound/Lights/Effects committee meets	Paul & Amy
2-Mar	General Meeting/Updates from Committees	Everyone
6-Mar	Committee work	Everyone
9-Mar	Committee updates/work	Everyone
16-Mar	Help Advertising committee make banners/flyers	Everyone
20-Mar	Help Props committee on final prop painting	Everyone
30-Mar	Committee work	Everyone
3-Apr	Post flyers and banners, presell tickets	Everyone
6-Apr	Committee updates/work	Everyone
10-Apr	Committee updates/work	Everyone
13-Apr	Dress Rehearsal	Everyone
17-Apr	Prepare stage	Everyone
20-Apr	Final Dress Rehearsal	Everyone
22-Apr	Set up for the show, audience, concessions	Everyone
23-Apr	SHOWTIME!	Everyone
24-Apr	SHOWTIME!	Everyone
25-Apr	Wrap Party	Everyone

You will need to make a **detailed schedule** for your event. Include everything that needs to be done. Figure out how much time each task will take. Set a start date for each task that is early enough for the task to be finished by the event date.

Make sure everyone agrees on what they are responsible for. Hold meetings to talk about the progress of each task. If someone is behind, see if he or she needs help. Everything has to be done on time, or you won't be ready by the day of the event.

Getting the Word Out

Okay, you've decided on an event. Now how do you get the word out so people will come? There are different ways to do it.

BANNER

Make a banner for your event. Include the name of the event, the location, and the date and time. Write big! People should be able to read it from a distance.

Hang your banner where a lot of people will see it. You may need to ask permission before hanging it. If you hang it outside, put it somewhere that it won't get wet.

WORD OF MOUTH

Let as many people know about your event as you can. They'll tell other people, and those people will tell more people, and so on.

Make Your Own Banner

1 Draw a sketch of the banner on a piece of paper. Be sure to include all the information about the event.

2 Cut a piece of banner paper the length the banner should be. You might want to measure the place where you plan to hang it.

3 Copy your sketch onto the banner paper. Use pencil so you can erase any mistakes.

4 Trace over the writing with a thick black marker or black paint.

5 Use colored markers or paint to decorate the banner. Make it colorful so people will notice it!

6 Hang the banner with masking tape.

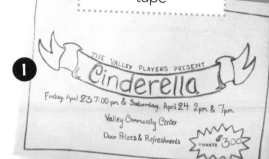

1

THE VALLEY PLAYERS PRESENT

Cinderella

Friday, April 23 7:00 pm & Saturday, April 24 2pm & 7pm

Valley Community Center

Door Prizes & Refreshments

TICKETS $3.00

5

THE VALLEY PLAYERS PRESENT

Cinderella

Friday, April 23, 7:00 pm. & Saturday, April 24, 2 p.m. & 7 p.m.

Valley Community Center

TICKETS $3.00

Door Prizes & Refreshments

The Valley Players Present

Cinderella

Friday, April 23
7:00 p.m.

Saturday, April 24
2:00 p.m. and 7:00 p.m.

Valley Community Center
100 Any Street

Tickets $3.00
Door Prizes • Refreshments

Posters are a great way to advertise your event. Your poster should include the name of the event, the type of event it is, when and where it is being held, and how much the tickets cost.

Hang posters where a lot of people will see them. Be sure to ask permission before hanging a poster. Some places have bulletin boards where you can hang posters:

* apartment building lobbies
* stores
* community centers
* schools
* places of worship

Make Your Own Poster

1 Design a **master** copy of your poster on a sheet of white paper.

2 Use bright colors so your poster will stand out. If you plan to use a black-and-white copier, use black on the master, and copy it onto colored paper.

3 Remember that copiers won't copy anything written too close to the edge of the master. So leave a border of at least ¼ inch (½ cm) on all sides.

4 Make as many copies of the master as you need.

WHAT YOU'LL NEED

white paper

black pen

markers or colored pencils

ruler

copier

colored paper (optional)

Money Matters

Let's face it. A big reason to have an event is to make money! There's nothing wrong with that. Here are some hints about money.

THE TREASURER

One person should be in charge of the money. Decide which of the event planners will be the treasurer.

The treasurer's job has two parts. He or she keeps track of how much is spent organizing the event. And he or she adds up how much the event earns.

This job is a lot easier if you set and follow a budget. A budget is a plan for how you will spend and earn money.

THE BUDGET

First, figure out the expenses. List everything you have to buy for the event. Find out what everything on the list will cost. Add up the amounts. That is the total you need to organize the event. Add a little extra for things you may have forgotten.

Next, figure out the income. How much money do you think your event can make? If you are charging admission, how many tickets do you think you can sell? What would be a fair price for the tickets? How much do you think you can make selling **refreshments**? How else can you make money at your event?

EXPENSES

Props/Costumes	HAVE	ESTIMATED PRICE	ACTUAL PRICE
Paint	X		
Gems			
Glue		$3.00	
Cotton balls	X		
Glitter	X		
Makeup		$2.00	
Fabric		$20.00	
Fliers/Banners/Signs		$20.00	
Banner paper			
Markers		$7.00	
Paint	X		
Paper for flyers/tickets	X		
Tape		$15.00	
Copying the flyers/tickets	X		
Refreshments		$20.00	
Popcorn			
Salt for the popcorn		$20.00	
Bags or boxes for popcorn	X		
Bottled water		$4.00	
Soda		$5.00	
Cookies		$12.00	
Apples		$10.00	
Napkins		$4.00	
Tablecloth		$4.00	
Miscellaneous	X		
Tickets			
Pizza for the crew	X		
		$25.00	
TOTAL EXPENSES		**$179.00**	

INCOME

INCOME	ESTIMATED INCOME	ACTUAL INCOME
Ticket sales 75 @ 3.00/each		
Refreshement sales	$225.00	
Popcorn 20 @ 1.00/each		
Soda 20 @ .50/each	$20.00	
Apples 10 @ .75 each	$10.00	
Cookies 30 @ .50 each	$7.50	
Bottled water 25 @ 1.00	$15.00	
	$25.00	
TOTAL INCOME	**$302.50**	

INCOME	ESTIMATE	ACTUAL
LESS EXPENSES	$302.50	
PROFIT	-$179.00	
	$123.50	

Sample form: make yours fit your business!

PROFIT OR LOSS?

If the income is more than the expenses, you will make a profit. If the expenses are more than the income, you will lose money doing the event.

Do you think you can make more than you spend? You won't know for sure until after the event. But you will have a better chance of making money if you figure your expenses and income accurately.

One way to increase your profit is to spend less on expenses. Make as many of the things you need as you can. See if you have any of the things you need for the event at home. Can you reuse or recycle **materials** to make what you need? Ask for permission before you use something for your event.

Save money by shopping at **garage** sales and **thrift stores**. Ask friends and neighbors if you can borrow things for the event.

TICKETS

Selling tickets is a good way to help manage the money at your event.

Tickets are especially helpful for events where people pay for more than just admission. You might also have a **refreshment** stand. Or maybe you're having a carnival with games people can play.

Set up one place to sell tickets for everything. Then all the money will be together. That makes it much easier to keep track of your sales.

Decide how much the tickets should cost. The admission tickets will cost the admission price, of course. Food or game tickets could each cost a certain amount, such as 25 cents. Then have people pay for things with the tickets. For example, you could charge one ticket to play a game. And you could charge two tickets for a cookie at the refreshment stand.

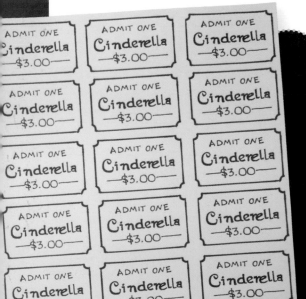

MAKE YOUR OWN TICKETS

You can buy tickets at party stores, but why not make your own? You can draw them or make them on a computer.

Create a **master** sheet of tickets. Make as many copies of the master sheet as you think you'll need. Cut out the tickets. Don't cut up the master sheet. You might need to make more copies.

You can make one kind of ticket for admission to the event. Make a different ticket for people to use for refreshments or games.

SELLING REFRESHMENTS

People like to eat! Selling **refreshments** is a great way to make extra money at your event.

You could sell foods such as popcorn, candy, and cookies. Offering healthy snacks such as fruit or nuts is also a good idea. Don't forget drinks, such as bottled water, juice, or soda! Look for things that are on sale. You could also try making refreshments, such as lemonade or brownies.

You might also need napkins, paper plates, plastic glasses, or other supplies. When you decide how much to charge for the refreshments, figure in the cost of the supplies. And add a little bit extra for your profit!

Then make sure people have an opportunity to buy the refreshments. If your event is a performance, include an intermission.

HANDLING MONEY

Be ready to make change for people buying tickets. Have extra five-dollar bills, one-dollar bills, and coins. If someone gives you a large bill, leave it out while you count the change. That way you won't forget what bill you are making change for. It's a good idea to have a cash box with a lock on it. Someone should always be with the cash box. When you are done selling tickets, put it in a safe place.

It's Show Time!

Are you and your friends interested in music or theater? You can put on a show and charge admission.

SHOW IDEAS
play or skit
talent show
music concert
dance recital
magic show
puppet show
variety show

BEFORE YOU BEGIN

Meet with the people interested in putting on the show with you. Select a type of show. Base it on the talents and interests of the members of your group. See pages 6–9 for tips on planning your show.

Create a budget for your show. See the example on page 15. Decide on a fair price for the tickets. How many people are likely to attend? How much do you think they'd agree to pay? Charge enough to make at least as much as you will spend.

Decide what date and time to put on the show. Make sure everyone working on the show can come on the show date.

Advertise the show so you get a large **audience**. See pages 10–13 for advertising ideas.

Make tickets for the show like the ones on page 16. You can sell some tickets in advance.

EVENT TIPS

∗ Save money on **props** and costumes by using things you find around the house. Don't forget to ask permission!

∗ Have plenty of chairs for your audience. You could also ask people to bring their own folding or lawn chairs.

∗ Search at the library or online for information about putting on a show.

∗ You can never practice too much. So practice, practice, practice!

DONATE
Give part of the profits to a charity. Tell people you plan to do this. Then you can choose a percentage of the profits to give.

PUT ON A PLAY

You and your friends can act in your own play! Check the library for a play that everyone in your group likes. Or try writing your own play.

CAST AND CREW

Figure out who will do what. Do you have enough people for all the parts? Can some people play two parts? Make sure you have enough people to handle the lights, sound, and special effects, as well as ticket and concession sales.

COSTUMES AND PROPS

Decide what you need to make the costumes and **props**. Be creative. This is an area where you can have a lot of fun. Remember, you are creating an illusion for your **audience**. Nothing needs to be perfect!

LIGHTS, SOUND, AND SPECIAL EFFECTS

Think about what kind of lighting will work for your play. Do you need spotlights? Is the play serious? Is it scary? Is it funny? Maybe colored lights would set the right mood.

Find some music that will work for the opening and closing of the play. Or, maybe you need music for a scene in the play. You can probably find recorded sound effects at the library or online.

ADVERTISE, ADVERTISE, ADVERTISE!

In order to make any money, you need an audience. Anyone can put on an event, but if people don't attend, you won't make any money. Make sure all the cast and crew have handed out flyers to everyone they know. Make sure to hold the play at a time that most people are able to attend.

Hold a talent show open to people of all ages. You might be surprised at the things your friends, relatives, and neighbors can do.

FIND THE TALENT

Make a flyer asking people to sign up to perform. Include the time, place, and cost to enter the show. Keep the entry fee low so you can get more talent.

SET A TIME LIMIT

Set a time limit for the performances. Each person should have an equal amount of time. During rehearsals, use a timer to make sure each person stays within the time limit.

GET AN AUDIENCE

Advertise the talent show like you would advertise for other shows. Use word of mouth, flyers, and banners. Give flyers to each performer. They can let all their friends and family members know about the show.

MAKING MONEY

Charge admission to the people attending. Have an intermission so the **audience** can buy **refreshments**.

Try having a few door prizes. People like a chance to win a prize! Have them write their names on pieces of paper when they arrive. Put the names in a box or bag. At the end of the show, draw names to win the prizes.

21

Haunted House

Hosting a haunted house is basically just putting on a spooky show. Don't be afraid to try it!

R. I. P.

~ HERE LIES ~

~ THEODORE FRIPP ~

HE HAD AN UNFORTUNATE SLIP.
HIS TIME ON EARTH
WAS JUST A BLIP.

R.I.P.

Sally Rae

783 – 1820

BEFORE YOU BEGIN

Get a group together to plan the haunted house. Where will you hold it? It could be in a **garage**, basement, or yard. You must get permission to use the space. When you have permission to use a location, begin planning. See pages 6–9 for tips on planning your event.

Create a budget for your show. See the example on page 15. Figure out how much to charge for admission. It should be enough to make at least as much as you will spend.

Decide what dates and times your haunted house will be open. Make sure everyone involved can be there when it is open.

Advertise the show. Put some **props** and a sign advertising the haunted house in your yard. See pages 10–13 for more advertising ideas.

Make tickets for the haunted house like the ones on page 16.

FEEDBACK
Ask your customers what they liked and didn't like. Use their ideas to make your next haunted house even better!

EVENT TIPS

* Consider who will be your **audience**. Will it be older or younger kids? You don't want to make it too scary for the little ones. But it should be interesting enough for the older kids.

* Choose a theme for your haunted house. It could be all about monsters or skeletons. Or maybe it's a creepy hotel or a haunted hospital. Use your imagination.

* Draw a map of the space. You'll need an entrance and an exit. Plan what spooky things you can do along the way. How many characters will you have?

* Make a path for people to walk through. You could use sheets or large pieces of cardboard for the walls.

* Be safe! Make sure everything you plan is safe. The actors shouldn't touch or hurt the customers. Keep all of the paths clear.

GRAVEYARD

Have your customers walk through a graveyard to get to the haunted house.

Make **tombstones** with funny or scary sayings. For example, one could say "I told you I was sick!"

Make the graveyard look old and overgrown. Put bunches of old, dried flowers by the tombstones. Stretch fake cobwebs around the tombstones.

Light it up! You want people to be able to see the graveyard at night. String holiday lights around the area. Put electric candles in carved pumpkins.

Stuff some old clothes to make a dead body. Add a skeleton if you have one.

Make a Creepy Hand

Stuff a glove and a shirt sleeve with rags or newspaper. Pin the glove to the cuff of the sleeve. Push a stick into the sleeve and stick it in the ground. Make a little pile of dirt around the hand. It will look like the hand is reaching out of a grave.

CONSTRUCTION AND PROPS

Decorate the doorway. Hang long black streamers or strips of black plastic from the top.

Hang empty picture frames. Have scary characters stand behind them. They can "come to life" and scare people.

Put fake cobwebs in the corners or on **props**. Add some glow-in-the-dark spiders or bats!

Hang long pieces of black thread from the ceiling. It will feel like walking through cobwebs.

Look in local stores for Halloween supplies.

SOUND AND LIGHT

A haunted house should sound scary. Find some creepy music and sound effects. Search online, or go to the library or stores with Halloween supplies.

Lighting can make a big difference. Try using colored lightbulbs. Don't make it too bright. Darkness is scary! Black lights make some things glow in the dark.

You can also buy glitter paint or glow-in-the-dark paint. Use it to make some creepy **props** or characters shine.

Flashing lights can cause some people to have **seizures**. So if you use them, hang a sign outside the haunted house that says there are flashing lights. That way your customers will know before they enter.

Backyard Carnival

Almost everyone loves a carnival. Gather a few friends and put on a carnival at your house!

POP CORN

BEFORE YOU BEGIN

It takes a lot of planning to put on a carnival. Have a planning meeting with everyone who wants to help out. Decide where to hold the carnival. Ask if you can have it in your backyard or **garage**. See pages 6–9 for tips on planning your event.

What carnival games will you have. What will you have for prizes? Will you have other entertainment? What **refreshments** will you offer?

Create a budget for your carnival. See the example on page 15. Figure out how much to charge for the games and refreshments. It should be enough to make at least as much as you will spend.

Buy or make tickets for the games and refreshments like the ones on page 16.

Advertise your carnival so a lot of people will know about it. See pages 10–13 for advertising ideas.

EVENT TIPS

* Test the games before the event. They shouldn't be too easy or too hard.

* Try using different rules for different ages. Let younger kids stand closer or try more times than older players. Or have separate games for different ages.

* Have different levels of winners for each game. For example, everyone who tries a game could get a small prize. Anyone who wins a game could get a larger prize.

* Make sure all of the games are safe. Don't set the games up too close together. Do not have any games that use sharp objects, such as darts. You should have an adult close by in case of an **emergency**.

Here are some game ideas to get you started. Use your imagination and make up some other games too. Look online or at the library for more ideas for games and prizes.

PLASTIC BOTTLE RING TOSS

This is a pretty easy game to make. Wash and save plastic water and soda bottles. When you have about 20 or 30 of them, tape them together. Decide what to use for rings. Small bracelets or large rubber bands work well. Or you can make rings out of wire. Leave the caps on the bottles. Give a special prize for tossing a ring around a bottle that has a certain type of cap.

CUPCAKE WALK

Write the numbers 1 through 10 on large sheets of paper. Tape them to the floor in a circle. Then write the numbers 1 through 10 on small pieces of paper. Fold them up and put them in a jar or basket.

Have ten people play at a time. Each person starts out standing on one of the numbers on the floor. Play some music. Tell the players to walk around the circle of numbers while the music plays.

After about a minute, stop the music. Each person should stop walking and stand on a number. Draw a number from the jar or basket. The person standing on that number wins a cupcake!

GO FISH

This is a fun game, especially for little kids. Make some fishing poles out of wooden **dowels**. Tape the end of a piece of string to one end of each dowel. Tape a spring clothespin to the other end of each string.

Give each kid a fishing pole. Have the kid throw the clothespin over a curtain. Someone behind the curtain puts a prize in the clothespin. Then he or she gives the line a couple of tugs. The kid pulls the line back over the curtain to catch the prize. Look for toy fish or other water-theme prizes for this game.

GUESS HOW MANY

Fill a jar with something small, such as jellybeans or buttons. Count them as you put them in the jar. Close the jar tightly.

Charge people for a chance to guess how many things they think are in the jar. Provide small pieces of paper for them to write their guesses on. Make sure they also write down their names. Collect all of the guesses in a basket or box.

At the end of the carnival, sort the entries. Find the one with the closest guess. That person wins a grand prize! More than one person might have the closest guess. So have two prizes or something that can be divided between the winners.

Tips for Success

Success isn't measured just by how much money you make on an event. How the event turned out is also important. Did the people who came have a good time? Will they come to other events you organize?

PLAN, PLAN, PLAN

Planning is the most important part of putting on an event. Plan every **detail** of your event, from idea to cleanup.

BE DEPENDABLE

Complete any task you agree to do on time. The event will only be a success if everyone does his or her part.

BE ON THE SAFE SIDE

Follow safety instructions. Make sure all areas of your event are safe.

BE POLITE

Respect your customers. Be friendly and thank people for coming to your event. Be respectful even if you don't agree with someone.

REVIEW

After the event, have a meeting to review how it went. What worked? What didn't work? Take notes to use when planning your next event.

THIS IS JUST THE BEGINNING

Okay, it is the end of the book. But, it is just the beginning for you! This book has provided information about some ways to make money. Now decide what might work for you. Talk it over with your parents. And don't forget to have fun!

Glossary

audience – the people watching a performance such as a play or concert.

detail – a small part of something.

dowel – a round rod or stick.

emergency – a sudden, unexpected, dangerous situation that requires immediate attention.

garage – a room or building that cars are kept in. A *garage sale* is a sale that takes place in a garage.

master – an original copy that is reproduced to make more of the same thing.

material – the substance something is made of, such as metal, fabric, or plastic.

prop – an object that is carried or used by an actor in a performance.

refreshment – food or a drink.

schedule – a list of the times when things will happen.

seizure – a sudden attack of muscle spasms or twitches.

thrift store – a store that sells used items, especially one run by a charity.

tombstone – a marker, usually made of stone, placed where someone is buried.

volunteer – to offer to do a job, most often without pay.

Index